About the Book

A CANADIAN BIRD lays its eggs each year in the days between May 26 and May 29. The morning-glory flower opens each day at sunrise and closes as the sun sets. Trees add a new ring to their trunks each year. Living things wake, sleep, eat, grow and migrate to the rhythms of built-in clocks. All these changes are measures of the passage of time. It's usually more convenient to measure time by changes everyone can observe, changes in the sun and the moon. And anything that moves or changes at a steady speed can be used as a clock: sand slipping through the narrow neck of an hourglass, a candle burning down, or a metal spring as it unwinds to move the hands of a wrist watch.

Using fascinating observations and activities, which can be performed by children for themselves, Melvin Berger's clear and thoughtful explanation of what time is and how it can be measured, and Richard Cuffari's accurate and engaging drawings will excite the curiosity and imagination of young readers.

TIME AFTER TIME

by Melvin Berger

illustrated by Richard Cuffari

COWARD, McCANN & GEOGHEGAN, INC.
NEW YORK

General Editor: Margaret Farrington Bartlett
Consultant: Theodore D. Johnson
          Montclair Public Schools

Text copyright © 1975 by Melvin Berger
Illustrations copyright © 1975 by Richard Cuffari

All rights reserved. This book, or parts thereof, may not be reproduced in any form without permission in writing from the publishers. Published simultaneously in Canada by Longman Canada Limited, Toronto.

SBN: GB-698-30558-2
SBN: TR-698-20306-2
Third Impression
Library of Congress Catalog Card Number: 74-83012
PRINTED IN THE UNITED STATES OF AMERICA
06209

TIME AFTER TIME

　Imagine that you live in a very special house. It has no doors. It has no windows. There are no clocks or watches. There are no radios or TVs. How can you tell time?
　Your body can help you keep track of time. Time after time it wakes you up in the morning and makes you sleepy at night. Time after time it makes you hungry.
　It is as though your body has a built-in clock. Your body's inner senses measure time. Chemicals inside your body make your built-in clock run. These chemicals change and move about. They make certain things happen time after time. They wake you up and make you sleepy. They make you feel hungry when it is time to eat.

All plants and animals have inner clocks. These clocks control the growth of living things. They make other changes take place in plants and animals.

Many trees lose their leaves at the same time every year.

Robins, ducks, geese, and other birds fly south in the fall and fly north in the spring.

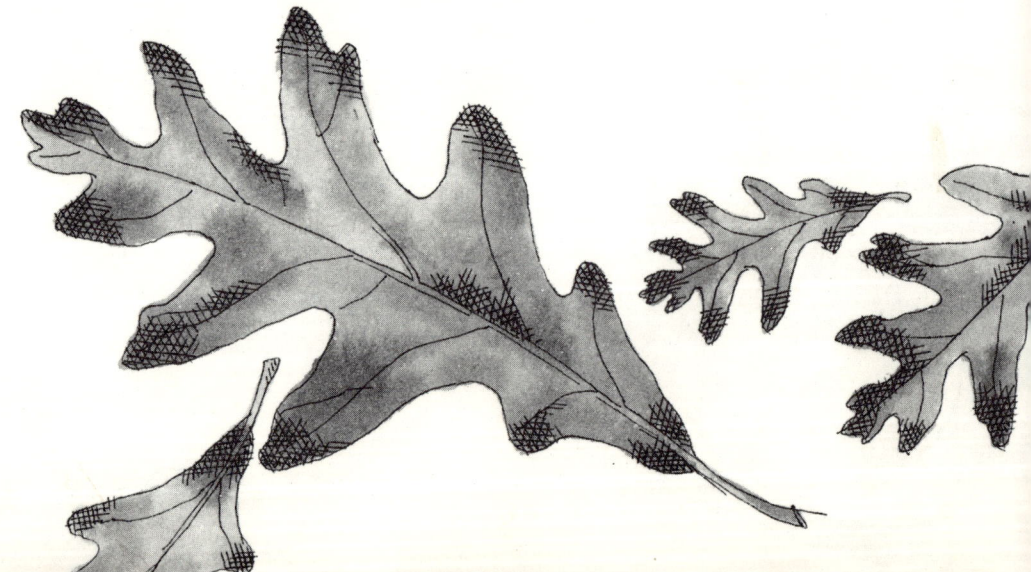

   The inner clocks of some animals and plants are quite amazing.

   Every year a Canadian bird, the greater yellowlegs, lays its eggs in the days between May 26 and May 29.

   The morning-glory flower opens as the sun rises. It closes as the sun sets. The four-o'clock, another flower, opens as the sun sets. It closes when the sun rises the next morning.

   Every year the swallows of San Juan Capistrano, California, fly south about October 23, and return about March 19.

We can see changes in living things that show the passage of time.

Each year a layer of new wood grows within the trunk of a live tree. These layers form rings in the trunk. When a tree is cut down, you can count the rings in the stump. The number of rings tells you how old the tree was when it was cut down.

The teeth of a horse show how old it is. It takes five years for a horse to grow all of its teeth. They never stop growing. So—the length and condition of the teeth tell whether a horse is just a colt or old enough to be put out to pasture.

The inner clocks of living things make them change and do things time after time. But we do not measure time by these changes. We use other changes in nature. We use changes that can be seen and used by all people.

We use the sun to measure time. When we see the sun rise, we say it is morning. When the sun sets, it is evening. We call the time from one sunrise to the next a *day*.

Of course, the sun does not really rise, move across the sky, and set. It just *seems* to move.

You know that the earth is always turning around. It is like a giant slow-moving merry-go-round. On a turning merry-go-round it sometimes feels as if you are standing still. Other

things seem to be moving around you.

From the turning earth it feels as though we are standing still, and the sun is moving. We see the sun come into view and move across the sky. Then we lose sight of the sun. As the earth keeps turning, the sun comes into view again.

We see changes in the moon, too. One night the moon is round and full. It grows slimmer each night until it disappears. Then a golden, thin curved line appears. Every night it grows fuller and rounder.

After many nights, it is a round, full moon again.
 We know that the moon does not really change shape. It is always a globe. But, looking up from earth, it *seems* to change.

When sunlight strikes the whole side of the moon that faces the earth, we see a full moon. As the moon moves in its orbit around the earth, less and less of the moon is lit by the sun. Finally we see no light on the face of the moon.

Then, as the moon continues to move around the earth, sunlight again strikes the moon. Little by little the moon seems to grow. Finally we see the full moon again.

So the moon also measures time for us. It takes about thirty days from full moon to full moon. We have named this length of time for the moon. It is called a *month*.

Just as the moon orbits around the earth, so the earth travels around the sun. For the earth it is a longer trip. It takes a longer time. It takes twelve months for the earth to make its journey around the sun.

During this journey the light and warmth from the sun cause the seasons on earth. The four seasons are spring, summer, fall and winter. Then it is spring again. The four seasons come back in the same order time after time as the earth follows its path around the sun.

Make believe that a straight line runs up and down through the center of the earth. This line is called the axis of the earth.

The axis of the earth tilts. All the time that the earth moves around the sun the earth axis tilts so that the north end always points towards the North Star. No matter where the earth is along its path around the sun, the axis keeps the same tilt. It

points to the North Star.

During part of the journey, our northern part of the earth is tilted towards the sun. Then daylight lasts longer. The sun's rays are more direct and feel warmer.

When we are tilted away from the sun, daylight becomes shorter. Then the sun's rays are less direct. They feel less warm.

We cannot see the earth's axis. We cannot see the earth moving around the sun. But we can feel what happens. We can see many of the signs of changing seasons.

For three months of the journey, it is the spring season. Seeds sprout. Plants grow. Birds find nesting places. Brooks are filled with water. Insects come from their hiding places.

The earth continues its journey. The summer season begins. The weather becomes hot. Flowers bloom. Fruits ripen. Hay is cut and stored. Dark clouds bring summer thunderstorms.

During the following three months days grow shorter. The weather is cool. Many trees lose their leaves. Some birds fly south. Seeds form on the plants. It is fall.

The earth moves on. For half of the earth the weather becomes cold. It is the winter season. Snow covers the mountains and many valleys. Animals find shelter from the cold. It is a resting time for plants.

After the winter is over, it is spring again. It takes twelve months, or about 365 days, for the earth to make one complete trip around the sun. It takes the same time for the four seasons—spring, summer, fall and winter—to pass. The four seasons are also a measure of time. We call this period of time a *year*.

Years, seasons, months and days are marked by changes in the sun and moon. But how can we measure parts of a day?

A shadow stick can measure smaller units of time. When a stick is set into the ground, the sunlight casts a shadow. The shadow moves as the sun moves. You can measure the hours of a sunny day by watching the moving shadow.

Here is a way to make your own shadow stick. First, you will make a square clock face. Start with a square piece of paper, about 8 inches long and 8 inches wide. Fold the paper in half. Open it up, and fold it in half the other way. Open up this fold, too.

At the top of the fold write the number 24. At the right end of the cross fold write the number 6; at the left end write the number 18. In the upper right corner write the number 3; in the lower right corner write the number 9. In the lower left corner write the number 15 and write 21 in the upper left corner. Now fill in the numbers in-between. The clock goes from 1 am to midnight, representing a 24 hour day.

Take your paper and a long, sharp pencil outdoors on a sunny day. Place the paper on flat ground. Push the point of the pencil through the paper where the two folds cross. Push it into the ground so that it stands straight up.

Now look at a clock or watch. Where is the little hand? Twist the paper so that the shadow of the pencil points to the same place. Watch your shadow stick for a while. Can you see the shadow move?

Look again a few hours later. Has the shadow moved? What time does it now show? Is it approximately the same as the little hand on the clock or watch?

Did you see any change in the length of the shadow? The shadow is very long just after sunrise. It grows shorter during the morning. At noon, when

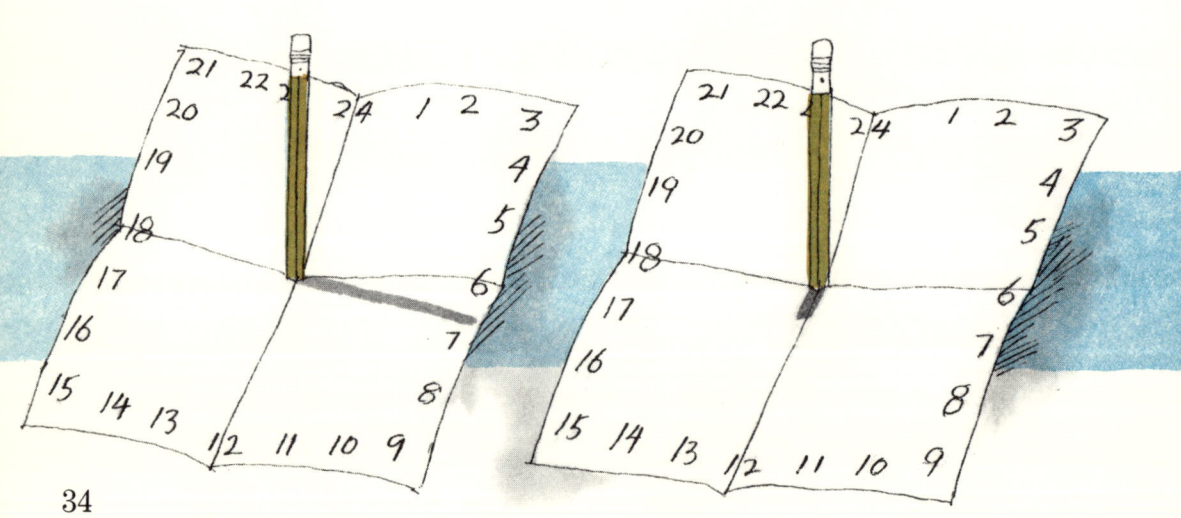

the sun is overhead, the shadow is shortest. During the afternoon it grows longer again. It is very long just before the sun sets.

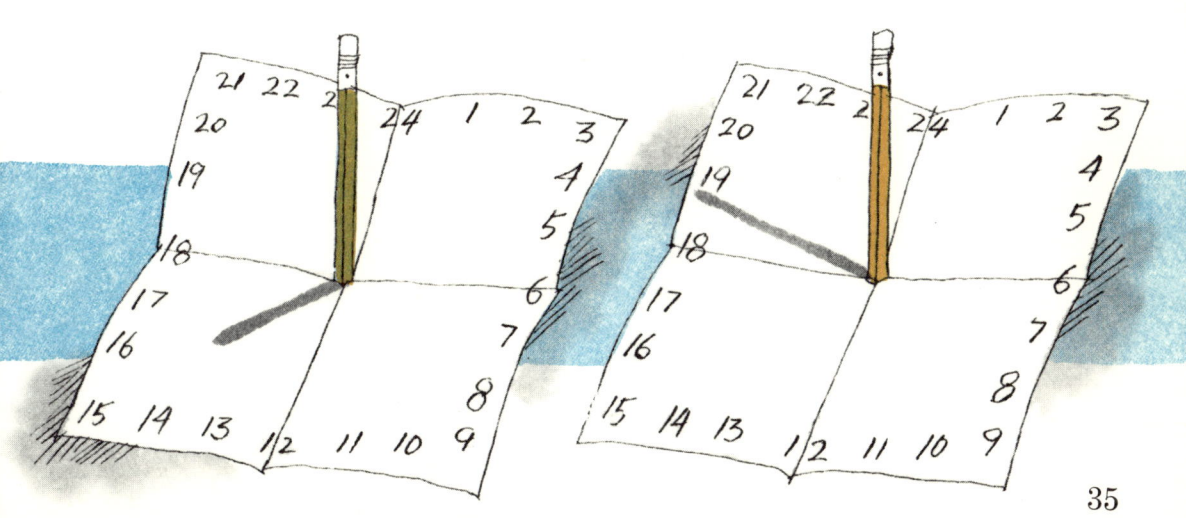

The shadow stick was the first clock. Later, better clocks were made. They became very important to people. Clocks help people to do things together. Can you imagine going through a whole day without a clock? Your body's built-in clock would tell you when to wake up, eat and go to sleep. But how would you meet your friends at the movies or get to your Scout meeting on time?

All clocks are the same in one way. They all have something that moves or changes at a steady speed, without getting faster or slower.

The early water clock measured time by the drip-drip-drip of water from a bowl. The time it took for the bowl to empty was an hour. In an hour, the candle clock burned down to a mark made on the candle. In the hourglass, it took an hour for sand to pass from the top of the glass to the bottom.

When you wind a watch or clock, you tighten a metal spring. The spring unwinds slowly. As it unwinds, it moves the hands of the watch or clock. In an electric clock, pulses of electricity move the hands.

The most modern clocks use atoms to measure time. Atoms are the tiny units of which all things are made. They vibrate, or shake back and forth, very quickly. An atomic clock is the best time keeper we have. It will not gain or lose a second in 30,000 years!

We keep learning more about time. We find that time is different in different places. When our side of the earth faces the sun, it is day for us. But for

the people on the other side of the earth, it is night. When we are waking up in America, there are people in China who are just going to sleep.

Our feeling of time also changes. Hours speed by when you are playing and having fun. Minutes seem like hours the day before summer vacation or when you stand in line waiting for an ice cream cone!

Although we know a lot about time, there is much more that we wonder about. When did time begin? Will time ever end? Does super-fast space travel change time? If the atom is the smallest unit of matter, what is the smallest unit of time? What new discoveries will we make about time?

Who knows? Only time will tell!

INDEX

Atomic clock, 41
Axis of the Earth, 24–26

Built-in clocks, 7. *See also*
 Inner clocks

Candle clock, 38
Clocks, 37–41

Day, definition of, 14

Electric clock, 41

Fall, 8, 23, 28, 29
Four-o'clock flower, 11

Greater yellowlegs, 11

Horse, age of, 12
Hourglass, 38

Inner clock, 8, 11, 14

Migration, 8, 11
Morning glory flower, 11
Month, definition of, 21

North star, 24–25

Seasons, 23–29
Shadow stick, 30–37
Spring, 8, 23, 26, 29
Summer, 23, 27, 29

Trees, 8, 12

Water clock, 38
Winter, 23, 29

Year, definition of, 29

About the Author

A graduate of University of Rochester, Melvin Berger did graduate work at Teacher's College, Columbia University, and at the University of London in England. He has many years experience as a public school science teacher.

Mr. Berger has written many scientific articles for magazine publication and a number of science books for children, including *Computers*, *Stars*, *Gravity*, *Atoms*, and *Storms*, which are all part of the *Science Is What and Why* series. Two of his books, *Oceanography Lab* and *The New Water Book* won recognition as Outstanding Science Books of 1973.

He lives in Great Neck, New York, with his family.

About the Artist

Richard Cuffari studied art at Pratt Institute. He has illustrated over fifty books for children, including *Little Yellow Fur*, *Who Will Wash the River?*, *Who Will Clean the Air?*, *Nothing Is Impossible*, and *Escape From the Evil Prophecy*, a Children's Book Council Showcase book for 1973. He has won awards from the Society of Illustrators and the American Institute of Graphic Arts for his work.